THE GOD KIND OF MARRIAGE

THE GOD KIND OF MARRIAGE

Bishop.Dr. William Wood

Wood World Missions Publication
Wood World Missions
238-240 London Road
Mitcham
Surrey,
CR4 3HD

ISBN-13: 978-1999919566

Printed in England

CONTENTS

Introduction. vii

1. The Christian Marriage 1

2. The Value of Prayer 35

3. The Principles of Prayer and Intercession ... 43

4. God is Able To Answer Our Prayers 62

INTRODUCTION

For a number of years now, I have wanted to write a book on this subject. I have been married now for over twenty years. However, I do not claim to be an authority in this area – but I know a man who does. He is God, the one who instituted marriage.

Over the years, I have learnt a lot about marriage and I believe that what i have shared in this book will bless all those who choose to read it.

As you read this book, it is my prayer that the Lord will bless you richly. If you are already married, it is my prayer that the contents of this book will open your eyes to some truths, which will enhance your marriage. If you are yet to embark upon the institution of marriage, it is my prayer that you will find this book as a very useful preparatory material.

I will however like to remind you that there can be no substitute for the Word of God. Read this book alongside with the Word of

God and allow God to prepare your heart for this great God ordained institution.

I have also included in this book some information on prayer without which no marriage would flourish. I also believe that this book can be a blessing to any Christian who has embarked upon a relationship with Jesus. Every relationship needs God, prayers and faithfulness. As you read this book, may the Lord use it as a tool to secure your marriage, your life, bring you closer to Him and strengthen your relationship with God.

It is my prayer that after reading this book you will come to realise that the God-kind of marriage is filled with Love, joy, peace, trust, prayer, patience, faithfulness, hope and victory. If any of these Godly attributes are missing from your marriage, then begin to cry out to the Lord for the missing piece of the puzzle to be returned to its rightful place in order for your marriage to stand strong. May the grace of God be sufficient for us all as we embark upon this journey of life.

In the final chapters you will find help on how to pray not only for a successful marriage but in other life circumstances. I believe this will richly bless you in your daily walk with the Lord.

I would like to thank Ivor and Janet Patnelli for finding the time to read this manuscript prior to publication.

Stay blessed as you read this book.

—Rev. Dr. William Wood
LLB (Hons) BL; Dip.MT
(Solicitor-Advocate)
©2008, (c) 2017, © 201

CHAPTER 1

THE CHRISTIAN MARRIAGE

Marriage is a God ordained institution; therefore anyone who embarks upon marriage must know God in order for their marriage to succeed. Anyone who embarks upon marriage without God is setting themselves up to fail.

From the onset can I make it absolutely clear that the God kind of marriage is the marriage that God instituted in the Garden of Eden. In this kind of marriage, God created one woman (Eve) for one man (Adam). I would like to call this kind of marriage the Christian marriage. Before I go any further, I will like to ask a question.

Who is a Christian?

A Christian, I believe, is someone in whose life the image of Christ is formed.

In Churches today we have a lot of believers and very few Christians. The Bible says even the devil believes and trembles. What God is looking for today are true Christians in whose lives the image of Christ is   reflected. In the Church of God today, we have the "visible congregation" and the "invisible Church". We must aim to be a part of the "invisible Church."

In the church of God today, a number of us are using the Christian terminologies but not many of us are doing the things that please God. The Bible says the Lord knows them that are his. We need to do the things that please God. It is only then that we can be confident of belonging to God's Kingdom.
In Galatians 4:19 Paul encourages us to travail with the Word of God until Christ be formed in us. It is the formation of Christ in us that makes us Christians. Paul also said in Ephesians 4:11-13 that we need to persevere in the Word of God until we all come to the unity of the faith.

In Philippians 3:10, Paul says "that I may know him and the power of his resurrection". In that scripture Paul wanted to experience the fullness of the measure of the Lord Jesus Christ. That must be our objective. We all need to ask God to teach us all we need to know about marriage before taking the plunge.

In Acts 11:26 the disciples were called Christians for the first time in Antioch. People saw them and recognised that they had been with Jesus. When people see us today, do they recognise that we are with Jesus? That must be our aim – to know God and to share him with those around us.

1 Peter 4:16 encourages us to be prepared to suffer as Christians for the sake of the Gospel of Christ. This means that as Christians we must be prepared to endure any suffering that comes as a result of being married.

What is it that Makes Us Christians?

In order for one to be a Christian, one needs to:

1. Believe in the finished work of Christ on the cross – *John 1:12*.
2. Receive Jesus as Lord and personal Saviour.

3. Allow Christ to be formed in us –
   Galatians 4:19.
4. Love God
5. Obey God by keeping His
   commandments - *I John 3:24; I John 5:18
   & Philippians 2:12.*
6. Allow the Holy Spirit to bear witness
   with our spirits that we are Sons and
   Daughters of God – *Romans 18:16.*
7. Allow our life to affect and influence
   those around us.
8. Be as Bold as Jesus, Peter and John –
   *Acts 4:13; Acts 8:9-24 & Acts 11:20-21 &
   26.* Jesus was and still is our perfect
   example.
9. Put off the old man and put on the new
   man – *Ephesians 4: 20-32*
10. Be ready to teach and proclaim the Word
    of God – *Matthew 28.*
11. Be prepared to suffer for the sake of the
    Gospel – *1 Peter 2:21-23.*
12. Be relevant to our communities both
    spiritually and socially.

If we are to enjoy the benefits of a true
Christian marriage, then we need first of all to
be the Christians that God expects us to be.

It is only then we will be able to enjoy the benefit of a true Christian marriage.

In effect, anyone who wants to get married without embracing Christ is wasting his or her time. Embarking upon marriage without Christ leads to failure.

When God created Adam in the book of Genesis, he declared that it was not good for a man to be alone. As a result, God created Eve to be "a help meet" for Adam. Genesis 2:18-25 makes this clear. Matthew 19:6 also states that when God created Adam and Eve, he intended for them to be one flesh. In Mark 10:9 the Bible says what God has joined together, let no one put asunder. All the scriptures I have quoted so far make it quite clear that God ordained marriage and he approves of marriage.

When a Christian gets married, it is important to recognise that marriage is more than just a wedding ceremony. It is in reality a welding ceremony. The Bible says that what God has joined together let no one put asunder. The Bible encourages husbands in Ephesians 5:25 to love their wives as Christ loved the Church and gave himself for it. This really means that there is nothing the wife will do that the husband should not be prepared to forgive. Getting married as a Christian is a divine ordinance. We need God's help and guidance to succeed in our Christian marriages.

In every marriage, there will be moments of pleasure and moments of pressure. If the parties in the marriage hold on to God and apply his word in their marriage, their moments of pressure will bring them together rather than pull them apart. For this reason, it is very important for a Christian to marry someone who has the same seed of God in them.
Reading the following scriptures will assist you greatly in this regard – Deuteronomy 7:3; 2 Chronicles 20:37; Nehemiah 13:3; Deuteronomy 22:10; Joshua 3:6-7; Isaiah 52:11 and Joshua 23:10-13.

How Many Wives Can a Christian Have?

A Christian can only marry one - Matthew 19:6 & Genesis 4:19a.

A number of Christians look at the life style of David and Solomon as recorded in 1 Chronicles 14:3 and 1 Kings 11:3-8 and wonder why they cannot marry as many wives as David and Solomon did. The truth is that you and I are in a different dispensation from that of David and Solomon. We are of the new covenant; they were of the old covenant. We as Christians are not allowed to have more than one wife.

What factors must a Christian consider in order to determine their readiness for marriage?

1. Maturity

A. ***Physical Maturity:*** - Before any Christian begins to consider marriage, they need to be physically matured. By physical maturity, I mean they must be old enough to get married. It is therefore not wise for a child or a young person to consider marriage while they are physically immature. At this point I am sure you will like me to tell you the age at which I consider an individual to be physically mature. It is not for me to tell you the age of physical maturity. All I can say is that in some countries people are considered to be physically mature when they are eighteen. In other countries it is twenty-one. One point I will like to stress is that the fact that an individual is eighteen or twenty-one does not make them automatically ready for marriage. A Christian must develop the attributes of maturity before actively considering joining the noble and God ordained institution of marriage.

B. ***Spiritual Maturity:*** - Before one considers the question of marriage, they must make sure that they first have a relationship with the creator of marriage. It is important that anyone who contemplates marriage must have Jesus as Lord and Saviour of their life. For any marriage to succeed, there must be the *agape* God-kind of Love present in the couple. The best way to learn how to love with the agape (love that transcends all boundaries) kind of love is to have a relationship with the God who has the gift of walking in Love. Love is an ingredient that must be present in any marriage if it is to succeed.

a. **<u>Financial Maturity</u>**:- Anyone considering marriage must ensure that they are first of all financially secure. For anyone to contemplate marriage when they do not have any savings is like asking for trouble. I am not suggesting for a moment that anyone contemplating marriage must have thousands of pounds in their account. What I am suggesting is that they must have enough money to enable them make a healthy financial start in life at the point of marriage.

C. **<u>Have a Conviction that the one you are about to get married to is the Right person.</u>**

Before getting married to anyone, you need to be convinced that that person will enhance and edify your life. You must be able to say with certainty that this is the person you would like to spend the rest of your life with. If you cannot say that with certainty, it could well be that that person is not the right person for you. It helps if both parties have a steady source of income.

D. <u>Maintain purity in Courtship</u>

We are living in times when it is the norm to sleep with your partner before Marriage. It is unfortunate that even we, so called Christians have embraced this erroneous practice and we do not see anything wrong with it. There is nothing wrong with getting to know your partner as a person but the sexual part of things must be left until after the marriage. Many Christians' testimonies have been stained and soiled by the act of pre-marital sex. If we say that we are Christians and truly love God, then we need to stay pure sexually in courtship. Your body is the temple of the Holy Spirit which is in you - *1 Corinthian 6:19.*

E. <u>On the Wedding day</u>

Even on the wedding day, you need to have a personal conviction that the person you are about to get married to is the right person. You need to be sure, that what you are about to do is what you really want to do. The reason why this is so important is because once you get married, you need to understand that the Bible says, "what God has put together, let no one put asunder". That is why you need to be sure of the one you are about to marry.

On your wedding day, make sure that everything about your wedding brings glory to God. The drinks you serve must bring glory to God. If you serve people with strong drinks that cause them to misbehave and fight on the night of your wedding, will their actions glorify God?

Even the dress your wife wears on the day of your wedding must glorify God. I have attended a number of weddings at which the dress worn by the bride is designed in such a way as to expose her cleavage. How could that bring glory to God? As Christians we must know what is right and do what is right in the sight of our God. As Christians, the places we choose for our honeymoon must also bring glory to God. We need to go to places that would be sanctioned by God.

F. <u>Parental Consent</u>

It is important to pray to the Lord to let you have your parent's consent about your marriage. Today, a lot of people get married without the consent of their parents. It is important that anyone wanting to get married seeks parental consent and blessings before they get married. Parental blessing is very important. I am a parent myself and it will be very sad to see my son get married to someone I do not approve of.

Having said that, it is important to note that if you seek your parent's consent about your marriage, they must not withhold that consent unreasonably. If they withhold their consent unreasonably, you would have fulfilled your role but failure to seek your parent's consent at all is what is wrong.

G. <u>The Act of Sex</u>

As Christians we need to understand that sex is legal in marriage. It must be done properly and in the right way. We need to do it with honour, dignity and respect. The Bible says when God created Adam and Eve, Adam knew his wife (they had sex), and had children.

When God created Adam, he gave him a male organ. When God created Eve, he gave Eve a female organ. God did this because he wanted them to use those instruments in order to produce children.

One thing that we need to remember is that God created Adam and Eve not Adam and Steve. The Bible says in Romans 1:26-27 that "because of this, God gave them over to shameful lusts. Even their women exchanged natural relations for unnatural ones. In the same way the men also abandoned natural relations with women and were inflamed with lust for one another. Men committed indecent acts with other men, and received in themselves the due penalty for their perversion". One thing that we must be absolutely clear about is that the male organ was made for the female organ. God did not create a Man to sleep with a man. He created the man for the woman. We need to keep it that way in order to bring glory to God.

We need to remember that during sexual intercourse, God is there. After all, the Bible says God is everywhere. The Bible says to the woman in Genesis 3 that "unto thy husband will thy desire be". I Corinthians 7:2-5 also says sex must take place and must take place properly. 1 Peter 3:7 encourages the husband to honour his wife so that his prayers will not be hindered.

Today, many men and women in the church are walking around all confused because they lack adequate and gratifying sex life. They are confused and angry with their partners to the point that they are always quarrelling with each other. This must stop. Married partners need to have regular, blissful and satisfying sex. They need to find their common ground or come to an agreement as far as sex is concerned and keep that agreement. This will vary from couple to couple.

Further suggested scripture reading regarding this matter are: Genesis 38:9; Malachi 2:16; 1 Corinthians 7:2-5; 1 Peter 3:7; Romans 8:11; John 8:32 and Ecclesiastes 9:10.

H. <u>Communication in Marriage</u>

What God wants is for our marriages to be peaceful and joyful. Every marriage must have an open and effective communication. Married couples need to feel free to communicate their concerns with their partners and not feel afraid or uneasy about doing so. We also need to express our appreciation and love for our partners at all times.

I. <u>Finances in Marriage</u>

The husband and the wife must be one when it comes to the issue of finances. By this I mean the wife needs to know what is happening to their finances and Vice versa. In today's Church, certain wives do not even know where their husbands work let alone knowing what they earn. This is rather unfortunate. It is vital that marriage partners be one financially. The best way to do this is to have one joint account into which all their salaries go. That account can be used to take care of joint expenditures. Apart from this, I also encourage couples to have separate accounts into which allocated sums can be put so that if either party wants to surprise the other on special occasions, they can do so without going into the main account. This ensures that parties in the marriage maintain some independence in their finances.

Scriptures that assist in this regard are as follows: Acts 4:32; Luke 3:11; Hebrew 13:16 and 1 Timothy 5:8.

J. <u>Children & Our Responsibilities</u>

Both the husband and the wife must play their part and be responsible for the upbringing of their children. Both parties in the marriage must be responsible for the upbringing of their children. Both parties need to trust God together to bring up their children in the fear and in the knowledge of the Lord.

The Bible says except the Lord builds a house they labour in vain that build it. It also says Children are the heritage of the Lord and the fruit of the womb is his reward - Psalm 127:1-5.

K. <u>How to Deal with In-Laws</u>

The Bible encourages us to live peaceably with all men and women in as much as it is within our power to do so. This includes In-laws. The last thing any married person wants to do is not getting on with their in-laws. As Christians we must get on with our in-laws. We need to do all we can to live peacefully with them. Other general points to note are as follows:

1. Visit your in-laws only when it is absolutely necessary. This could be on festive occasions and other such occasions. In the African context, people visit their in-laws too often. The most important point is not to visit your in-laws more than is absolutely necessary.

2. Never report your partner to your parents
3. Never allow a third party into your marriage. The best people to discuss your marriage issues with are your partner, God or a well-trusted spiritual father or mother.
4. Do not quarrel with your in-laws
5. Do not say bad things about your in-laws even to your partner.
6. Do not condemn your in-laws even if your partner does so.
7. Do not confide in anybody about your in-laws.
8. Give your in-laws every deserved respect.
9. Keep your in-laws away from the affairs between you and your partner.
10. Be in good communication with your in-laws especially when it comes to issues about their personal welfare.
11. If possible, do not bring your in-laws into your home for too long unless it is absolutely necessary.
12. Keep a steady mind on your spouse. Do not concentrate more on your in-laws at the expense of your partner.

It is vital that both parties in the marriage agree to allow the Lord to grant them wisdom and guide them in their marriage. Both parties in the marriage need to agree to walk in the wisdom of the Lord in order to make their marriage what it ought to be. We need to be wise when dealing with our partners and our in-laws.

L. **<u>Christians and Divorce</u>**

The Bible says, "God hates Divorce". That is a statement, which I believe every married Christian needs to take note of. If we are truly children of God, then we need to ensure that we do not do anything that will displease our God.

The Bible says "Husbands love your wives as Christ loved the Church and gave himself for it". This means that there is nothing that the wife will do to the husband that the husband should not be prepared to forgive or vice versa. Christ loved us whilst we were in our sins. He loved us enough to forgive us. We are expected to do the same.

When it comes to the question of the Christian and Divorce, we need to remember that so far as God is concerned, Marriage must be a permanent experience – Matthew 19:1-12. Romans 7:2-3 also states that ideally, only death should dissolve any marriage.

Proverbs 3:5-6 says "trust in the Lord with all your heart, and lean not on your own understanding; in all your ways acknowledge him, and he shall direct your path". Brothers and sisters, if we trust in the Lord, he will direct our marriages and make it what it ought to be.

12: <u>What Are the Sources of Conflict in Marriages today?</u>

1. Failure to maintain communication within the marriage. Lack of information can be a source of conflict within the marriage.
2. Parties harbouring grudges and accumulating faults.
3. One party to the marriage taking decisions and acting on it without consulting the other party.

4. Delay in coming home consistently by one party in the marriage.
5. One party in the marriage feeling that they are not part of the family's decision-making process.
6. Failure to finish job started in the home.
7. Entertaining conflict situations within the home.
8. Lack of compliment of one another.
9. Not returning your partners phone calls.
10. Treating each other with contempt.
11. Parties not listening to each other's concerns.
12. Allowing other people to take your partners place.
13. Treating others better than you treat your own partner.
14. Attending more to the needs of your children at the expense of your partner.
15. Allowing the stresses of life to be brought into your relationship.
16. Failure to assist your wife in the home and with the welfare of the children.
17. Parties not being open and transparent with each other.

18. Parties promising each other and failing to keep their promises.
19. Parties lying to each other about various issues.
20. Parties ignoring each other's feelings and wishes.
21. Where either party in the marriage harbours the idea that they can live without the other.
22. Failure to resolve conflicts quickly when they arise.
23. Where one party in the marriage spends money without the consent of the other party.
24. Parties treating each other in a degrading manner.
25. Parties disgracing each other in public.
26. Parties undermining each other in Public.
27. Parties not showing respect for one another.
28. Parties disrespecting each other before their children.
29. Parties openly criticising each other in public.
30. Parties in the marriage ignoring each other both in public and at home.

31. Parties humiliating each other in public.

32. Parties giving each other excuses and refusing each other sex without good Biblical reason.

33. Parties failing to speak with one voice especially in public.

34. Parties lying to each other about financial matters and other project type matters.

35. Parties belittling each other in public. Parties not respecting each other.

36. Parties in the marriage not studying the Word of God together.

37. Parties in the marriage not praying together.

38. Not sharing the same faith with your partner.

39. Parties in the marriage not fellowshipping together.

40. Parties in the marriage failing to acknowledge their faults to each other.

41. Parties in the marriage promising to change when they do wrong and failing to change with the passage of time.

42. Excessive spending by either party in the marriage.

43. Not being sensitive to the needs of each other.

44. Either party doing their own thing within the marriage.

45. Either party doing things without regarding the effects on the other party in the marriage.

46. Parties not spending quality time together.

47. Parties in ~~to~~ the marriage feeling unwanted.

48. Parties not sharing the same interests.

49. Parties in the marriage being drawn apart from each other by circumstances.

50. Parties using their children as pawns in their home.

51. Parties failing to communicate effectively with each other.

52. Parties not taking each other's complaints seriously.

53. Parties dismissing each other's complaints outright and not taking each other seriously.

54. Parties refusing to find their common ground.

55. Parties refusing to deal with issues directly.

56. Parties refusing to deal with issues calmly.

57. Parties refusing to deal with issues thoughtfully.

58. Parties refusing to deal with issues considerately.

59. Parties refusing to deal with issues gently.

60. Parties refusing to deal with issues compassionately.

61. Parties refusing to deal with issues seriously.

62. Parties refusing to deal with issues prayerfully.

63. Parties not forgetting about issues that have been dealt with.

64. Parties allowing issues of concern to them to linger on rather than deal-with it.

65. Parties not allowing the Word of God to be the source of their common ground.

66. Parties sharing their concerns with others rather than with the party to whom they are married.

67. Parties not finding out why their partners are unhappy, feeling unfulfilled, feeling frustrated and feeling upset.
68. Parties in the marriage having different perceptions and expectations about their marriage.
69. One party in the marriage putting the other party's belongings in a black bin bag and throwing it outside the house.
70. Parties not doing things that will make the other partner consistently happy.
71. Parties not taking quality breaks together.
72. Parties not spending quality time together.
73. Parties not understanding how their partners are feeling.
74. Parties loosing their first love for each other.
75. Parties failing to allow the love of God to guide them in their marriage.
76. Parties not allowing the Love of God to step into their marriage when their own Love fails.
77. Parties not appreciating each other enough.

78. Parties allowing third parties into their marriage unnecessarily.

79. Parties valuing others more than the one to whom they are married.

80. Parties taking hasty decisions without first seeking the face of the Lord.

81. Parties failing to meet the very high expectations they have of each other.

82. Lack of forgiveness in the marriage.

83. Lack of trust between the parties in the marriage could also be a source of conflict.

84. Parties not recognising the effects of their negative actions on their partner.

85. Parties not recognising the effects of their inactions on their partner.

86. Parties assaulting each other verbally, physically and psychologically.

87. Parties refusing to speak to each other.

88. Parties in the marriage not listening to each other.

89. Parties not making their true feelings known to each other.

90. Parties not being truthful to each other.

91. Parties not being faithful to each other.

92. Parties in the marriage not expressing words of assurances to each other.

93. Parties being absorbed with negative details to the point of absurdity.

94. Parties blaming each other about everything that goes wrong or in some cases about things they fear are about to go wrong.

95. Lack of affection in the marriage.

96. Lack of tolerance in the marriage.

97. Parties not walking in the spirit.

98. Parties walking in the flesh.

99. Parties walking in selfishness.

100. Lack of affection in the marriage can also be a source of conflict.

How to Help Resolve Conflicts in the Marriage

1. Parties in the marriage must learn to listen to each other's concerns and do their best to resolve those concerns as best as they can. By listening I do not mean just hearing each other. I am talking about actively listening to each

other and assimilating what is being said.

2. Parties in the marriage must acknowledge each other's concerns. They must let their partner know that their concerns have been registered.

3. Parties in the marriage must assure each other that all concerns and issues that arise will be resolved through prayer.

4. Parties in the marriage must learn not to take things personally.

5. Parties in the marriage must avoid confrontation at all cost.

6. Parties in the marriage must not be aggressive, defensive or dismissive.

7. Parties in the marriage must avoid the habit of blaming each other for every potential challenge that arises.

8. Parties must learn to take responsibility for their part in whatever issues arise.

9. Parties in the marriage must learn to apologise for their part in any conflict situations that arise.

10. Parties in the marriage must learn to say sorry when it is required.

11. Parties must learn to love each other with the God kind of love.

12. Parties to trust each other.
13. Parties to be faithful to each other at all times.
14. Parties must be willing to change for the betterment of their marriage.
15. Parties to spend quality moments together as much as they can.
16. At the same time, Parties in the marriage should set aside quality time for each other and with God – the originator of their marriage.
17. Parties in the marriage must never assume that their marriage will last forever. They must constantly trust God and continue to work towards making their marriage what God wants it to be.
18. Parties in the marriage to cultivate the habit of praising each other often.
19. Parties to buy presents for each other every now and again.
20. Parties in the marriage to respect each other always.
21. Parties in the marriage to praise each other in private and in public.
22. Parties in the marriage not to demand more sex from their partner than their partner is able to offer.

23. Parties in the marriage to express their love for each other often.
24. Parties to avoid criticising each other in public and in private.
25. Parties in the marriage must respect and promote each other's call in life and Ministry.
26. Parties in the marriage must love the Lord with all their heart.
27. Parties in the marriage to value the partner God has blessed them with.
28. Parties in the marriage must trust God to give them the grace to get on with their partner.
29. Parties in the marriage must never think that they have married the wrong person. This is because what you think will affect what you do.
30. Parties in the marriage must never say to their partners that it was a mistake marrying them. This could have long lasting effects on the partner on the receiving end of such callous words.
31. Parties in the marriage must stop looking at other people and desiring them.
32. Parties must try their best to fulfil each other's expectations as best as they can.

33. Parties in the marriage must study each other and try to do the things that please their partner so long as what their partner likes is consistent with the Word of God. For example if you are married to someone that likes to steal, you have the right to say no to that kind of behaviour because stealing is not consistent with the word of God.

34. Parties must learn to be patient with each other.

35. Parties in the marriage must learn to fast and pray about the problem areas of their marriage.

36. Parties in the marriage must be determined that their marriage will work.

37. Parties in the marriage must trust each other.

38. Parties in the marriage must trust God for a Goodly and Godly Character.

39. Parties in the marriage must never forget that their marriage is God ordained and that no one is allowed to put it asunder except on the grounds of Adultery.

40. Even when one of the party has committed adultery, the other party in

the marriage must know that they have the option of forgiveness. The Bible encourages us in Matthew 18:21–35 to forgive them that sin against us. It goes on to say that God expects us to forgive others freely just as he forgave us. It will take the grace of God to do all of this and that is why we must always lean on God.

41. Parties in the marriage must fear God.

42. Parties in the marriage must value their marriage.

43. Parties in the marriage must love each other with the love of God.

44. Parties in the marriage must be determined to keep their marriage vows.

45. Parties in the marriage must never stop communicating with each other about their likes and dislikes. This must not be seen in the negative. It all helps to strengthen the relationship.

46. Parities in the marriage must know that marriage is God's idea – Genesis 2:18-24

47. Parties in the marriage must be committed to each other completely – Genesis 24:58-60.

48. Parties in the marriage must ensure that they bring into the marriage a good measure of romance – Songs of Solomon 4:9-10.

49. Parties in the marriage must know that marriage creates the best environment for raising children

50. Parties in the marriage must know that Marriage is a covenant and with every covenant we have as Christians, God expects us to fulfil our part of the covenant – Malachi 2:14b.

51.

<u>It is my prayer that God will make our marriages a living testament that will bring glory and honour to His name. Amen</u>

CHAPTER 2
THE VALUE OF PRAYER

We are living in times when we have need of prayer like we have never had before. I dare say marriage couples need prayer more than ever before. Today, the devil seems to have intensified his attacks on marriages. I dare state that the marriages that will succeed in today's world are the marriages committed and dedicated to God.

We have need of prayer today like we have never had before. In Matthew 26:40, Jesus asked His disciples the following question "could you men not keep watch with me for an hour"? Today, Jesus is looking forward to hear our prayers. Jesus our interceding high priest is praying for us. We his followers need to spend quality time in prayer if we are to succeed in our life and marriages.

Many Christians today do not pray. As a result most of our marriages need help. Our lack of prayer has also given the devil and his demons the chance to win contest after contest by default. We need to realise that our prayer plus Jesus' prayer equals victory.

Most married couples today are oblivious to the eternity shaping events that are happening around them and therefore do not realise the need to increase their prayer life and pray without ceasing.

As followers of Jesus sleep, Satan is winning the battle over many marriages. Many marriages today are experiencing the following:

- Failure
- Shortages
- Lack of love
- Lack of joy
- Lack of peace
- Ruined relationships
- Ruined lives
- Ruined reputations
- Broken homes and multiplied tragedies
- Unfulfilled dreams and visions.

Today most Christians are allowing interruptions, fatigue and pressures to drown out God's call on us to pray. Everyone, even married couples find excuses not to pray. For our marriages to succeed, we need to be a people of prayer. The Bible says in Jeremiah 33:3 that "… call unto me and I will answer thee and show you great and mighty things that you know not of."

Benefits of Prayer

When we pray:
- Our lives and our circumstances will change for the better.
- Something supernatural happens to us.
- It helps us to set, maintain and to pray God's priorities into our lives.
- It enables us to appropriate God's provisions for our lives.
- It enables our lives to move in a Godly dimension.
- It enables us to experience greater Joy and Peace in our lives.

- It enables us to experience fulfilment in our relationship with God and with one another.

- It enables us to walk in the realm of the spirit.

- It enables us to move in the Power of God.

- It enables us to stand in the victory that Jesus won for us two thousand years ago.

- It enables us to become the unified and determined force that God wants to see and use in these end times.

- It enables us to be transformed from being sluggish and disheartened followers of Christ into Bold and living witnesses for Christ.

- It transforms us into a mighty spiritual army for the Lord's use.

- It enables us to seize on difficulties and turn them into opportunities.

- It enables us to storm the gates of hell and take back everything that the devil has stolen from us. In Matthew 16:18 the Bible says when David sought the face of the Lord, the Lord responded by asking David to "pursue, overtake and recover all". Today if we will seek the face of the Lord our God, he will help us to recover all that the devil has stolen from us.

- It enables us to hear the voice of God and to know the will of God – Hebrews 3:7.

- It enables us to operate more effectively in the spirit realm – In Zechariah 4:6 the Bible says it's "not by might or by power but by the spirit of God". The desire to pray is not something we can work up in our flesh. The desire to pray is birthed in us by the Holy Spirit. God wants us to develop that desire for a daily discipline of prayer. God wants prayer to be a Holy delight to us and not a drudgery or cumbersome duty.

- It enables God to do mighty things through us. God wants his house (the Church and us) to be a house of prayer – Matthew 21:13 says God gets angry at a church that is not praying.

- It gives us an excellent spirit and enables us to stand God's corner and fight for him – Numbers 13:30 – end. (Joshua and Caleb). Prayer is so vital to the Church today that Jesus found time to teach his disciples how to pray. Prayer was a priority with Jesus. In Mark 1:35 the Bible says Jesus went to a solitary place very early in the morning to pray. If Jesus had to do this in order to succeed in his ministry, then we also need to pray in order to succeed in our lives, marriages and Ministries. Prayer must therefore be a priority for us if we are to be of any use to God here on earth. In Matthew 14:23 the Bible says after Jesus fed the 5,000 people he went up alone into a mountain to pray. Luke 22:39-41 also says Jesus went out as was his habit to pray. Jesus also taught his disciples to pray by Word and by his example. Jesus had cultivated the habit of prayer to the extent that when he was being jeered and ridiculed on the cross, he could think of nothing but offer a word of prayer to God for his jeerers and tormentors – Luke 23:34.

- It enables us to flow in the compassion and anointing of God. When we pray, we must not only pray for our needs, and ourselves we must constantly pray for others and their needs. We also need to pray for our families, our churches, our pastors and leaders, our nation and the leaders of our nations. This will enable us live a quiet and peaceable life – James 5:16; Jude 1:20; Psalm 122:6; Genesis 18 and 1

Timothy 6:12. We must also remember to pray for the harvest – Acts 2:47; Isaiah 43:5-7; Ephesians 2:2, Hebrews 1:13-14 and Matthew 9:37-38.

- It enables us to receive the fruits enshrined in prayer - Mighty Miracles, Authoritative Revelations, Wonderful Healings & Powerful Deliverances.

- It makes us unafraid even in the face of death – Luke 23:34 and John 19:30.

- It enables us to join our prayers with Jesus' prayers. This then has the effect of producing the answers that we require. Hebrews 7:25 confirm that Jesus is presently seated at the right hand of God making intercession for us. This shows that you and I are on Jesus' prayer list. When we pray, it enables Jesus' prayer request about us to come to pass.

- It causes us not to fall into temptation – Matthew 26:40-41 and Matthew 4:4.

- It enables us to spend time with God. We are living in times when we need to desire God and take delight in prayer like we have never done before. Prayer is so vital that Jesus spent time teaching his disciples how to pray – Matthew 6:9-13 and Luke 11:2 onwards.

- It enables us receive from God the desires of our heart. The Bible says in Psalm 37:4 that "if we delight ourselves in the Lord, he will give us the desires of our heart". This means that if we desire to see our marriages and life grow from strength to strength, we can see it happen if we seek the face of God in prayer.

- It enables righteousness, peace and Joy in the Holy Ghost to be made available to us. If we seek first the kingdom of God and his righteousness, all the things we need would be added to us.

From all that I have stated so far, it is quite clear that for us to see any success in our marriages and in our lives generally, we need to be a people of prayer. If we are to prayer effectively and effectually, then we need to be conversant with the principles of prayer and intercession.

CHAPTER 3

THE PRINCIPLES OF PRAYER AND INTERCESSION

In *Luke 18:1* the Bible encourages us to pray always. In order for our prayers to be effective, we need to know the principles that govern prayer and intercession.

1. The first principle we need to know about prayer and intercession is that it is to our benefit if we cultivate the habit of praying. We are living in times where everyone likes to talk about prayer. We need to desire to pray always. Our life must be a life of prayer.
2. We need to know the will of God through his word before we can pray effectively. We need to know what the word of God

says concerning every situation of life that concerns us.

3. We need to have the right attitude concerning prayer. We must know that grumbling and having a pity party does not get the attention of God.

4. We must know that faith in God's word is what gets God's attention. Faith pleases God. If we spend more time with God, our faith in him will grow.

5. We must know that every kind of prayer has rules. If we follow the rules, we will see answers to our prayers. There are different kinds of prayer: Prayer of faith, prayer of agreement, prayer of binding and loosing, prayer of intercession, prayer of worship, prayer of consecration and dedication, united prayer and prayer of commitment. I will address these in detail in due course.

6. God expects us to grow in our prayer life. If we do not grow in our prayer life, it will make us weak Christians. There is a saying that "a prayer less Christian is a powerless Christian but a prayerful Christian is a powerful Christian".

7. God expects us to put on the whole armour of God when we pray. This applies

to all kinds of prayer: the whole armour of God includes the following: Truth, righteousness, Being ready to preach the Gospel of peace, having faith, salvation, the Word of God and praying always.

8. Matthew 6:6 encourages us to Pray in secret. The Bible encourages us not to pray because we want to be seen praying. The Bible encourages us to pray in secret. We are encouraged to find a private place, shut the door to everything else other than God and pray to him fervently and without any distraction. The more we pray consistently and diligently, the more our attention and focus will be on our God who answers prayers.

9. When we pray we need to be God conscious. God wants us to concentrate on him and let our imaginations be fixed on him.

10. In prayer there must be an attitude of ferventness and seriousness. The Bible says in James 5:16 onwards that "the effectual fervent prayer of the righteous man availeth much".

11. When we pray, we do not necessarily have to be loud. God hears quiet as well as loud prayers. The most important thing is that

our prayers must be sincere. The Bible says Elijah was a human being like us. But when he prayed earnestly, seriously and sincerely, he got results. Today you and I can get results to our prayer if we pray earnestly, seriously and sincerely. Elijah had already heard from God so he was able to pray fervently believing in what he was praying about. His mind was set on God and God's ability to answer him. When we pray like Elijah did, something will happen in the spirit realm.

12. We are spirit beings and must be in contact with the spirit realm. Prayer enables us to do just that. When Herod threw Peter into prison, the Bible says the church offered fervent prayers for him. God heard their prayers and answered them. Today God will do the same thing for you and I.

13. When we pray, we need to watch out for the things that can hinder our prayers from being answered. These hindrances include the following:

- Unforgiveness - *Mark 11:25-26*

- Unbelief – *Hebrews 11:6*

- Unconfessed Sins – *1 John 1:7-9; Isaiah 59:1-2*

- Asking with the wrong motives – *James 4:3*
- Not praying in line with the word of God – *James 4:2-3*
- Not praying in faith – *2 Kings 20:1-6*

TYPES OF PRAYER

The Bible encourages us to pray without ceasing in 1 Thessalonians 5:17. In order for us to do this effectively, it is important that we know which type of prayer will be efficacious at any given time. Prayer can be defined as being in contact or communion with God.

Before I discuss the types of prayer, I want you to understand that prayer is the will of God. God expects us to pray. God wants us to have him on our mind always. He wants us to talk to him everywhere. Ephesians 6:18 encourages us "…to pray always with all prayer and supplication in the spirit, and watching thereunto with all perseverance and supplication for all saints".

1. <u>The Prayer of Binding and Loosing</u>

Matthew 18:18 says whatsoever we bind on earth shall be bound in Heaven and whatsoever we loose on earth shall be loosed in Heaven. This means that we have the power to bind and to loose. In other words, whatsoever we prohibit, heaven will stand with us and whatsoever we allow, heaven will stand with us. We need to understand that Satan is not afraid of us **per se**. He is always afraid of who we represent. If we submit ourselves to God and resist the devil, the Bible says he will flee from us.

As Christians we must be quick to repent of our sins if we want to flow with God always. We need to stand on the Word of God always when we pray. We need to continuously and consistently study God's word if we are to employ God's word in our prayers. As Christians, we always need to be on our guard. We need to bind the works of the devil and to loose the works of God in our lives – Luke 13:16. We need to be loose from our bondages. As we declare ourselves loose, God will back us up and we will be loose in deed from our bondages.

2. <u>Prayer of Agreement</u>

Matthew 18:19-20 says if two or more people are in agreement in prayer, they shall accomplish much. God guarantees this in his word. We need to believe God's word and to act on it. With prayers of agreement, all those praying in agreement must be in agreement concerning the issue being prayed about.

Deuteronomy 32:30 says the power of God is multiplied when two or more people pray together. When we pray, Satan will always come and say to us that our prayers will not be answered. Who will we believe, God or satan? It is up to us to believe what God has promised and see it happen in our lives.

If we truly believe God when we pray the prayer of agreement, we will begin to see changes in our circumstances.

3. <u>Prayer of Consecration and Dedication</u>

In Luke 2:39-46, Jesus prayed dedicating himself into the hands of the Lord. He was very focused on God when he prayed that prayer. When Jesus prayed the prayer of consecration and dedication, he was willing to surrender and embrace the will of God. When we are in unity with God, the power of God is able to flow through us. Jesus submitted to his father's will. We need to learn from Jesus and do the same consistently. We need to consecrate and dedicate our lives to do the will of God. The more we do this, the more others will be able to see Christ in us.

2 Timothy 2:15 encourages us to study the word of God in order to show ourselves approved unto God. If we know the will of God, we need to go ahead and act on it. The Bible says " and ye shall know the truth and the truth shall set you free". I suggest to you that the truth that you and I declare over our lives will surely set us free. The Bible also says in Romans 8:14 that those who are led by the

spirit of God are the true sons of God. Other scriptures that you can read in relation to this type of prayer are Matthew 26:39-44; Mark 14:35-41 and Luke 22:42.

One thing we need to know in this world is that "everything of God is supernatural but not everything supernatural is of God".

4. <u>Prayer of commitment</u>

This is the type of prayer, which enables you and I to commit our challenges and concerns into the hands of God. Whenever we pray this kind of prayer, we must not go back and worry about the same things that we have committed into God's hand. 1 Peter 5:7 encourages us to cast all our cares unto God because he cares for us.

Whenever we continue to worry about the issues we have committed into God's hands, it is like saying to God that we do not trust in his ability to deliver and sustain us. If we truly commit our ways unto the Lord, we will be able to enjoy the peace of God. Psalm 55:22 says we should "cast all our burdens upon the Lord". Psalm 37:5 also encourages us to commit our ways unto the Lord, trust in him and he shall bring to pass the answers we need to see. Philippians 4:6 also encourages us to be anxious for nothing but by prayers and supplications with thanksgiving we should make all our requests known unto God. It is only then we can begin to enjoy the peace of God.

Matthew 6:25 onwards encourages us not to worry. In fact whenever we worry, we are sinning against God. We need to repent of worry and begin to trust God. We can only smile at the storms if we have truly committed our ways unto the Lord. If we commit our ways unto the Lord, Psalm 112:7 says, "we will not be afraid of evil tidings". Daniel was not troubled when they threw him in the lion's den because he had already committed his life unto the Lord. Today if you and I will commit our concerns and issues unto the Lord in prayer, we shall see the hand of God move in our lives like we have never seen before.

Psalm 55:22 says God will sustain us if we cast all our burdens unto him. It is up to us to do what we need to do in order for us to receive the results we need to receive.

5. <u>United Prayer</u>

With united prayer, there is an element of agreement. The Bible says in Acts 4:23-31 that after Herod killed James he saw that it pleased the Jews. As a result he went on to arrest Peter also intending to kill him after the Passover. The Bible however goes on to say that Peter's prayer partners offered prayers to God. They prayed a united prayer. They prayed for Peter's release from prison. This was a humanly impossible task. But the Bible says God answered their prayers. As I join with you today in prayer, it is my prayer that God will sustain your life and marriage in Jesus name. Other scriptures you can read in this regard are Acts 12 and Acts 16.

6. <u>Prayer of Supplication</u>

The Bible encourages us to pray this kind of prayer. This is the kind of prayer that enables us to pour our hearts out to God. The Bible says in 1 Samuel 1 &2 that Hannah poured her heart out to God and God answered her cry. God will answer you and I if we develop the habit of pouring our heart out to him.

Another scripture that you can read in relation to this kind of prayer is Philippians 4:6 -9.

7. <u>**Prayer of Intercession**</u>

This is the kind of prayer, which enables us to stand in the gap for someone else and for others. In Genesis 18:16-33, Abraham stood in the gap for Sodom and Gomorrah. He wanted to know whether God would spare the land. On that occasion God did not spare the land of Sodom and Gomorrah because of their sins and wicked ways. Ezekiel 22:30-31 is another scripture that helps to explain this kind of prayer.

Prayer of intercession is hard work. However the more we desire to intercede for others, the lighter God would make our burdens. The Church also interceded for Peter in Acts 12.

Their prayer of intercession released the supernatural, which brought freedom to Peter. Moses on a number of occasions interceded on behalf of the children of Israel. (Numbers 14:11-20; Exodus 32:7-10; Exodus 32:11-14; Psalm 106:23; Micah 7:18; Ezekiel 33:11 and 2 Peter 3:9). We also need to cultivate the habit of interceding for others.

8. <u>Prayer of Faith and Prayer of Petition</u>

When we pray the prayer of faith it is the art of petitioning God by faith in accordance with his word. Whenever we pray the prayer of faith expecting God to answer, he will answer.

When we pray the prayer of faith, we must not waver. With this type of prayer we totally take God at his word and see that answers to our prayer come to pass right before our eyes.

It is the kind of prayer that enables us to grow in the things of God. As we pray the prayer of faith and see answers to our prayers, it moves us on to trusting God for our other needs and the needs of others.

When we pray in faith, we must expect to see results – first in the spirit realm and then in the physical realm. Whenever we pray in accordance with God's word, power is released into our situation and circumstances – 1 John 5:14; Mark 11:24 and Matthew 21:22.

When we pray the prayer of faith, we need to be expectant. Our expectancy will enable us to receive more from God. God will never let our expectations go unfulfilled. The expectations of anyone who prays the prayer of faith will always be realised.

9. <u>The Prayer of Worship</u>

This is the kind of prayer that enables us to minister unto the Lord in worship. The Bible says in Acts 16:25-34 that when Paul and Silas found themselves in their midnight situation, they praised and worshiped God. This is the most difficult thing that anyone without God could do. However, because Paul and Silas knew their God, they were able to offer Him the prayer of worship in the face of their difficult circumstances. What do you do in your midnight hour? Begin to offer God some worship and see his hand move in your life like you have never seen happen before.

The prayer of worship is the highest form of prayer – Acts 13:1-4. This is when you praise and worship God for who he is. *(Psalm 9 & Psalm 22).* When we do this, it brings the presence of God down.

10. <u>**Prayer in the Spirit**</u>

Jude 1:20 encourages us to pray in the spirit. In that scripture we are told that he who prays in the spirit edifies himself. This kind of prayer has also been referred to as praying in the Holy Ghost. 1 Corinthians 14:14-15 is another scripture that one can read in this regard. With this kind of prayer it is our spirit that prays, our understanding is unfruitful. In other words, when we pray this kind of prayer, we do not understand what we are saying to the Lord. When we cultivate the habit of praying in the spirit, we cannot go wrong.

Praying in the spirit has many benefits. Some of the benefits of praying in the spirit are as follows:

- It enables us to tune into the spirit realm better. *(Acts 2:4 & Acts 4:1 onwards)*
- We edify ourselves when we pray in the spirit. *(1 Corinthians 14:4)*
- It reminds us of the indwelling presence of the spirit of God. *(John 14:16-17)*
- It keeps our prayers in line with God's will. *(Romans 8:26-27)*
- It stimulates our faith. *(Jude 1:20)*
- It keeps us free from worldly contamination. *(1 Corinthians 4:26)*
- It helps us to pray for the unknown. The Holy Spirit prays through us. *(Romans 8:26-27)*
- *It gives us a* spiritual refreshing. It enables us to rest in God. *(Isaiah 28:11-12)*
- It enables us to give thanks perfectly. *(1 Corinthians 14:15-17)*
- It brings our tongue under subjection. The more conscious we are of God, the more we are careful about what we say. (James 3:8)

How to Pray Effectively

For us to pray effectively, we need to do the following:

- We need to pray in accordance with the Word of God, which is the will of God. This means that we need to abide in God and His word must abide in us. This will enable us to be effective in our prayers. The scripture that we can read with regard to this point is John 15:7-8.

  - We need to ask in the name of our Lord and Saviour Jesus Christ – John 16:23-24. We must always pray to the father through Jesus Christ.

  - God's word must abide in us richly – Acts 6:4 says God will always honour his word if we use it in our prayers – Psalm 138:2 & Psalm 119:105 & 130.

  - When we pray, we need to confess our sins – known and unknown. We also need to cultivate the habit of confessing our sins to one another. This means we must not be hypocrites. We must learn to speak the truth. We must also remember to pray for one another. We must not be selfish when we pray – James 5:16-18.

- When we pray, we must pray earnestly, sincerely and with confidence. (1 Kings 18:41 onwards).
- When we pray, we must pray with some seriousness – James 5:16-18
- When we pray we must be persistent in our prayers – Luke 11:5-13.
- When we pray, we must expect results. (John 15:7).
- When we pray, we must be specific about what we want from God.
- When we pray, we must resist doubt. (James 4:7).
- When we pray, we must find scriptures that guarantee us the answers to our prayers. (John 15:7-8)
- When we pray, we must believe that we have the answers by faith.(Mark 11:24).
- When we pray, we must meditate on God's promises. (Joshua 1:8 & Philippians 4:8)
- When we pray, we need to mix it up with the spirit of thanksgiving. There is a saying that a heart that is full of praise and thanksgiving keeps the devil at bay. (Philippians 4:6 & Romans 4:7-22)
- Pray continuously and in faith.

- When we pray we must remember that God delights in showing us mercy and he desires to meet our needs. (Micah 7:18)

The Bible says he who has ears to hear must listen to what the spirit of God is saying to the Church. We are the Church of God. Let us take note of all that God is teaching us and apply it in our lives so that we can reap the full benefits of effective praying.

CHAPTER 4

GOD IS ABLE TO ANSWER OUR PRAYERS

The Bible says in Matthew 7:7 that "ask and it shall be given unto you, seek and you will find, knock and the door shall be opened unto you". Revelations 3:20 also says "behold I stand at the door and knock, if anyone hears my voice and opens the door, I will come in and sup with them".

As Christians we must not give up easily. We must know at all times that God is omnipotent. He is an all-powerful God who has all that we could possibly need. We need to seek his face in prayer about all our needs. Some of the things we could seek the face of God for are things like:
- ➤ Our Lives
- ➤ Our Ministries

- ➤ Our marriages
- ➤ Our jobs
- ➤ Our children
- ➤ Our finances
- ➤ Our protection
- ➤ Our children
- ➤ Our visions
- ➤ Our dreams
- ➤ Our healing and deliverance
- ➤ Our peace
- ➤ Our joy
- ➤ Our future and much more.

As Christians, we need to believe in the omnipotent and omniscient God—who caters for our needs and is able to answer our prayers. With some of us who call ourselves Christians, deep within our hearts we really do not believe that God is capable of handling the prayer requests that we bring to him. This must change. We need to understand that:

- • God created the world including us.
- • He loved us despite our sins and sent Jesus to die on the cross to save us from our sins.
- • He is able to raise the dead.
- • He is still able to heal the sick.

- He is able to calm every stormy water in our lives.

Today he wants us to recognise that he is able to answer our prayer. As Christians we need to know and understand that God has power over the following:

1. __God Has Power Over Nature__.

- He parted the red sea – Exodus 14
- He parted the river Jordan – Joshua 3
- He provided food for his people – Exodus 16
- He caused bread and fish to multiply – Matthew 14:13-21 & John 6:1-13
- He stilled the storms – Mark 4:35-41
- He extended the daylight hours for his people in order to give them enough time to defeat their enemies – Joshua 10:12-14
- He provided water for his people when they needed it. He also provided water from the side of a dry rock when his people needed it – Exodus 17:1-7.

2. **<u>God Has Power Over Circumstances, Even Impossible Circumstances</u>**.

In Acts 12, the Bible says King Herod put Peter in prison. King Herod's intention was to kill Peter after the Passover. Herod placed sixteen Roman soldiers around Peter to guard him. This was an impossible situation. The only way Peter was going to get out of that place was through divine intervention.

The Bible tells us that Peter's company prayed for his deliverance. Whilst Peter was in this critical situation the Bible says, "he slept". This is the mark of a man who knows his God. He had no doubt that deliverance was coming. In the end Peter was miraculously released from his incarceration. Today if you and I will trust in the Lord, He will deliver us from every prison situation that the devil cares to put our way. Receive this word of prophesy in Jesus name. Today every Iron Gate in your life will be opened in Jesus name.

After Peter was released from prison, the Bible says in Acts 12:15-16 that the disciples and apostles who were praying for Peter's release from prison were astonished when they saw Peter at the door. Today may the Lord astonish you in Jesus name. May the miracle working power of God meet you at the point of your need in Jesus name.

3. <u>God Has Power Over Hearts</u>

The God we serve has the power to change the hearts of men and women and that of authorities.

- God was able to change the heart of Moses from being a shy person to a bold and confident leader – Exodus 3 & Exodus 4.
- God softened the heart of the cruel Pharaoh – Exodus 11:1-8
- God discouraged Elijah from quitting – 1 Kings 19:15
- God turned the fanatical persecutor, Saul into a globe-trotting Apostle Paul – Acts 9:1-31
- God turned the timid and cowardly Peter into the rock and the first major leader of the Christian Church – Matthew 16:18-19.

The Bible says God changes not. Jesus also never changes – Hebrews 13:8 & Malachi 3:6. God does not grow tied and weary. If he was able to do all these miracles for our brothers and sisters who have moved on before us, then he can do the same for us – Isaiah 40:28.

4.<u>God Has Power Over Sickness & Disease</u>

The word of God has countless number of stories of people who received their healing. Some of these people who received their healing are:

- The woman with issue of blood – Mark 5:25-34
- Jarius' daughter – Mark 5:21-24 & Mark 5:35-43
- The blind man – Mark 8:22-26
- Blind Bartimaeus – Mark 10:46-52
- The ten lepers – Luke 17:11-19.
- The impotent man – John 5:1-9
- The blind man – John 9:1-41.

5. <u>God Has Power Over Death</u>

In John 11, the Bible tells us that God was able to raise Lazarus from the dead. He was also able to raise his son Jesus from the dead. Today, Jesus is seated at the right hand of God making intercession for you and I. Whatever dead situation you face today, may the Lord raise it up for you in Jesus name.

6. <u>God Has Power to Protect His People</u>.

- God was able to deliver Daniel from the jaws of the lions in the lion's den – Daniel 6:20-22.
- God was able to save the lives of Shadrach, Meshack and Abednego – Daniel 3:17

7. <u>God Has Power to Perform Miracles</u>

- God was able to give a child to 90 year old Sarah and 100 year old Abraham – Romans 4:18-21

- God was able to feed 5,000 people
- God was able to turn water into wine – John 2
- God was able to provide his followers all their needs – 2 Corinthians 9:8

Brethren in Christ, I will like you to know that the God that we serve is able to save us completely when we come to him through Christ Jesus – Hebrews 7:25. God can do more than we can ever ask or think of or imagine – Ephesians 3:20. God wants us to come to him continually in prayer – 1 Thessalonians 5:17.

Today God is inviting the weary and the burdened to come to him – Matthew 11:28-29. If you are reading this book today, God is speaking to you. Take all your cares and worries to God in prayer. He will not only hear you, but he will answer you in Jesus name.

Habits We Need To Cultivate When We Pray

There are a number of habits we need to cultivate as we pray to God. I have indicated below some of the habits we need to cultivate. They are as follows:

- We must pray regularly
- We must pray sincerely
- We must pray privately
- We must pray publicly when required to do so
- We must pray specific and to the point prayers
- We must talk to others about prayer
- But most important of all we must pray. We need to "talk less and pray more" in Jesus name.
- When we pray we must follow the following order:

1. Adoration – 1 John 3:1
2. Confession – 2 Corinthians 5:17
3. Thanksgiving – Psalm 103:2 & 1 Thessalonians 5:18 and

4. Supplication – Philippians 4:6; James 1:5 and James 4:2.

Brethren, begin to pray and keep it up in Jesus name. May all the answers that are due you come to you as you pray in Jesus name.

- May the lord bless your life in Christ
- May the Lord bless your family
- May the Lord bless your home
- May the Lord bless your work
- May the Lord bless your business
- May the Lord bless your studies
- May the Lord bless your Ministry
- May the Lord bless your marriage and
- May the Lord bless everything that you do in Jesus name.

Stay blessed in Jesus name.

If this book has blessed you in any way, shape or form, we will like to hear your testimony. Simply write your testimony and send it to us.

Our postal address in the UK is:
Wood World Missions & Power Centre Church
238 – 240 London Road
Mitcham, Surrey, CR4 3HD, United Kingdom
E-mail:-
rev.dr.wood@hotmail.co.uk
or
woodworldmissions@hotmail.com
Website address:-
<u>www.woodworldmissions.org</u>
or
www.powercentrechurchuk.org
U.K.: Tel. No: (+44) 208 286 3018
Mobile: (+44) 7909 486 846
Ring any of the above numbers for information about the Wood World Missions' free Bible School in the United Kingdom.